THE WILD WORLD OF ANIMALS

THE WILD WORLD OF ANIMALS

CROCODILES

MARY HOFF

CREATIVE EDUCATION

Special thanks to Dr. Adam Britton, Wildlife Management International.

Published by Creative Education, 123 South Broad Street, Mankato, Minnesota 56001. Creative Education is an imprint of The Creative Company. Designed by Rita Marshall. Production design by Advertising & Design. Photographs by Alamy (La Belle Aurore, Danita Delimont, Chris George, Martin Harvey, ImageState, Geoffrey Morgan, Beren Patterson, Peter Arnold, Inc., Carole Robertson, Eitan Simanor, Raoul Slater, SUNNYphotography.com, Genevieve Vallee), Getty Images (Theo Allofs, Jose Azel, Gallo Images-Roger De La Harpe, James Warwick, Art Wolfe).

It is a hot summer evening in Lower Zambezi National Park in Zambia, Africa. A crocodile floats along in the water of the Zambezi River, only its eyes and nostrils visible above the surface of the water. After a few minutes, the crocodile sinks down into the river. It lurks there for a while, then sees a catfish in front of it. Pushing itself forward by wiggling its long tail, the crocodile lunges toward the fish. Underwater, the long, toothy snout opens and shuts. Snap! The fish has become a meal for this big, water-loving animal.

Crocodiles move quickly and quietly in the water   **5**

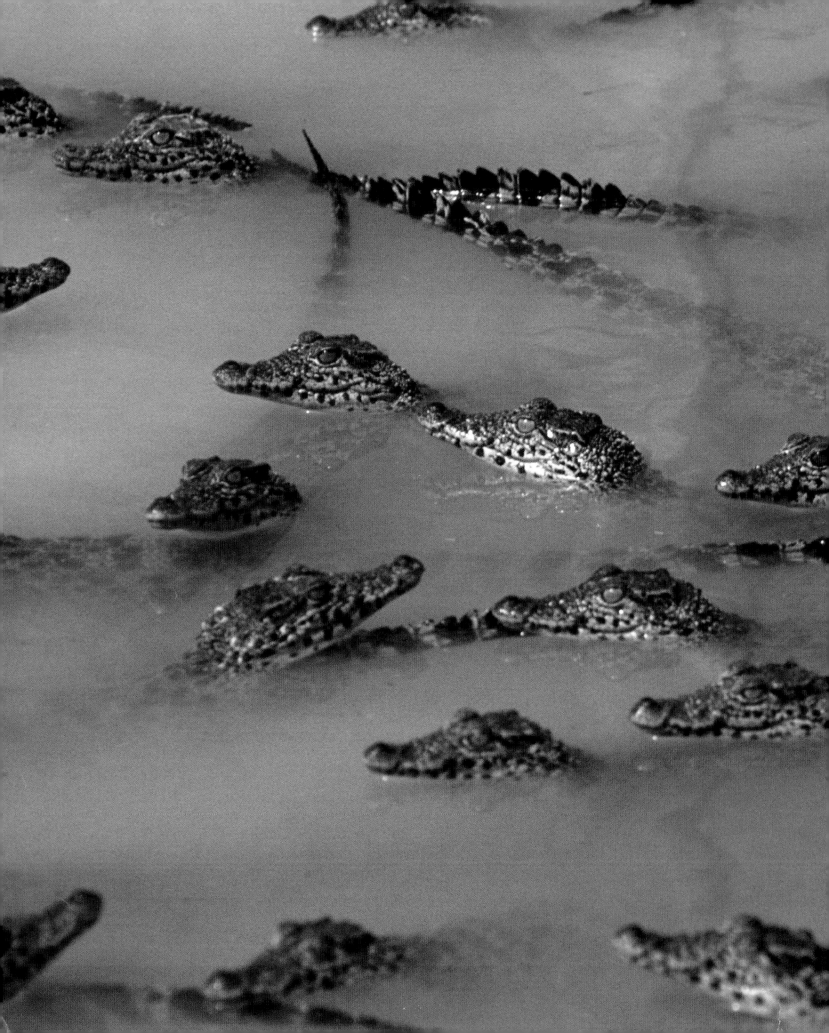

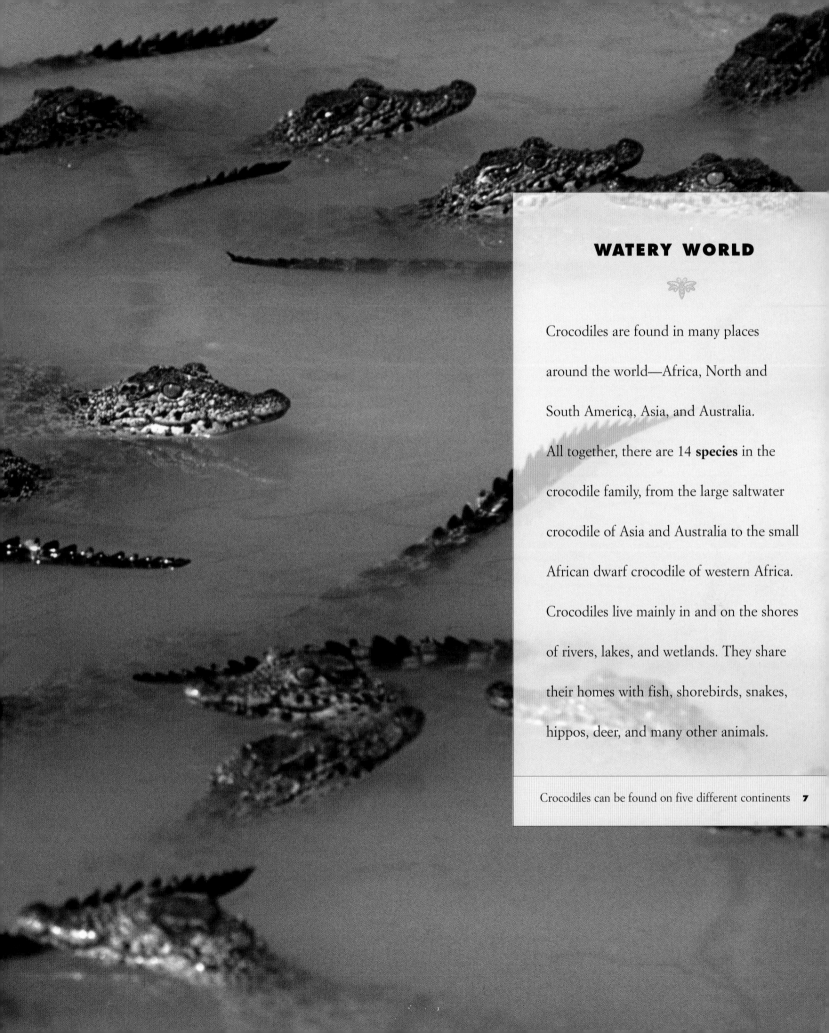

WATERY WORLD

Crocodiles are found in many places around the world—Africa, North and South America, Asia, and Australia. All together, there are 14 **species** in the crocodile family, from the large saltwater crocodile of Asia and Australia to the small African dwarf crocodile of western Africa. Crocodiles live mainly in and on the shores of rivers, lakes, and wetlands. They share their homes with fish, shorebirds, snakes, hippos, deer, and many other animals.

Crocodiles can be found on five different continents **7**

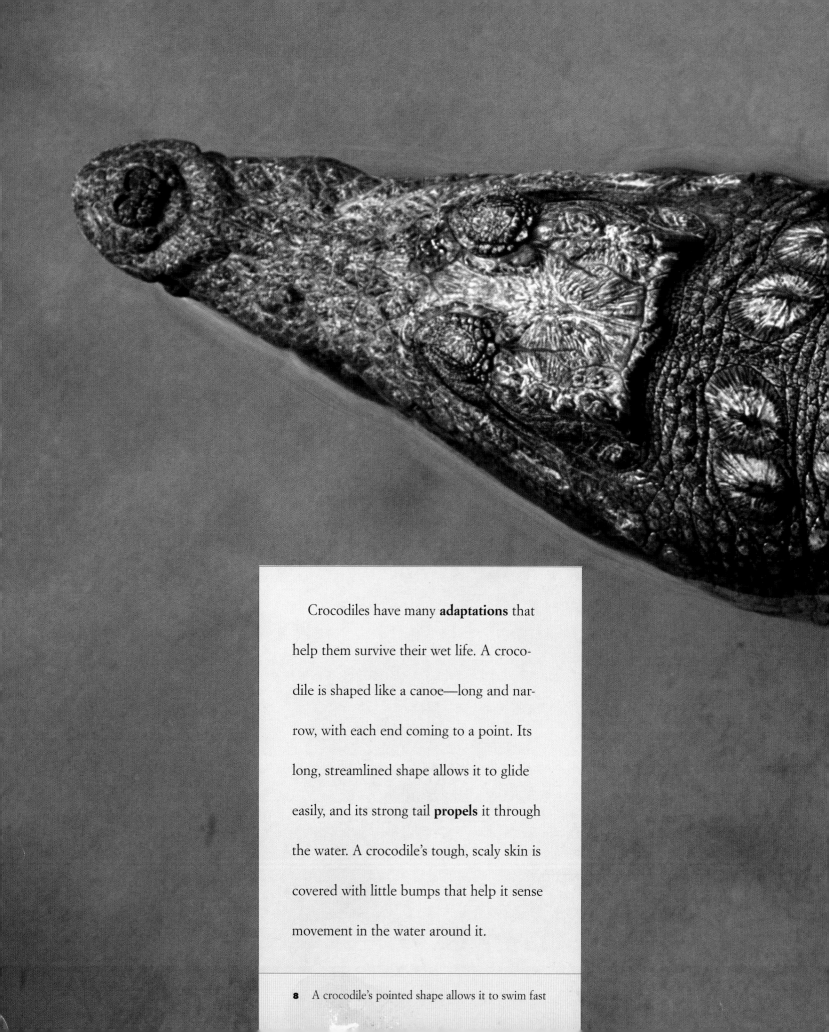

Crocodiles have many **adaptations** that help them survive their wet life. A crocodile is shaped like a canoe—long and narrow, with each end coming to a point. Its long, streamlined shape allows it to glide easily, and its strong tail **propels** it through the water. A crocodile's tough, scaly skin is covered with little bumps that help it sense movement in the water around it.

8 A crocodile's pointed shape allows it to swim fast

A crocodile's nostrils, ears, and eyes stick out from the top of its head. This lets a crocodile hide most of its body under-water but still see, hear, and breathe. A crocodile's eyes have see-through lids called nictitating membranes. They clean the eyes and keep them from getting scratched. At the back of its mouth, a crocodile has a special flap that keeps water from running down its throat and into its lungs. This prevents the crocodile from choking as it swims underwater with its mouth open to catch **prey**.

Crocodile jaws have bone-crushing biting power

Crocodiles are meat-eaters. They have big teeth and strong jaws that they use to capture, kill, and eat other animals such as fish or birds and **mammals** that come to the water's edge to drink.

Birds sometimes make a small meal for crocodiles

Crocodiles are **reptiles**. Like other reptiles, their body temperature changes with the temperature of their surroundings. When they are cold, they move into the sunshine to let its rays warm them. When they are too warm, they move into the shade or the water to cool off. When the weather turns very hot or very cold, crocodiles use burrows in riverbanks for shelter.

Crocodiles need the sun for energy and warmth **13**

Crocodiles grow throughout their lives and may weigh more than 500 pounds (227 kg). The saltwater crocodile can grow to be more than 16 feet (5 m) long—longer than a mini-van. But the dwarf crocodile grows only to a length of five feet (1.5 m).

Baby crocodiles are covered with dark spots and bands and bright yellow patches. Adults are usually tan with a lighter-colored belly, often with black patches.

The biggest known crocodile was 22 feet (6.7 m) long

LIFE AS A CROCODILE

A crocodile begins life inside an egg. A mother crocodile lays dozens of eggs in a hole, then covers them up with sand or plant material to keep them warm and protect them from lizards and other egg-eating animals. A couple of months later, the baby crocodiles are ready to hatch. They start making noises, and the mother digs up the eggs. She might even help the little crocodiles work their way out of their shell by rolling the eggs around in her mouth. When all of the young are hatched, she takes them to water.

Baby crocodiles are about eight inches (20 cm) long

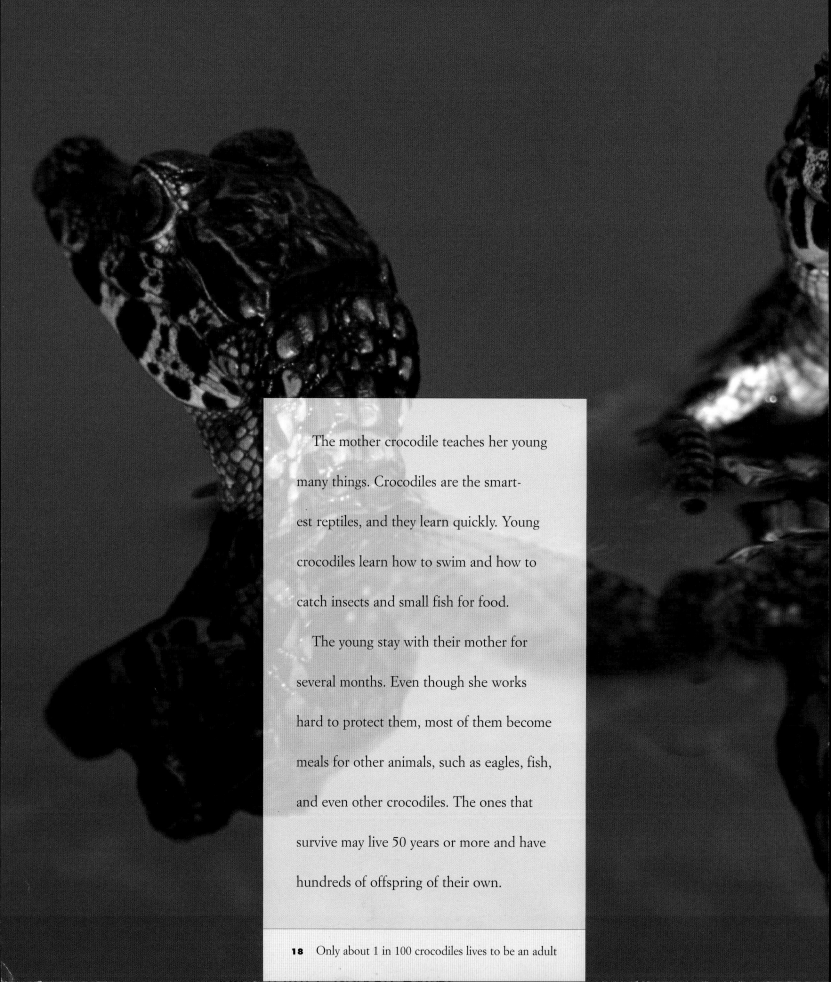

The mother crocodile teaches her young many things. Crocodiles are the smartest reptiles, and they learn quickly. Young crocodiles learn how to swim and how to catch insects and small fish for food.

The young stay with their mother for several months. Even though she works hard to protect them, most of them become meals for other animals, such as eagles, fish, and even other crocodiles. The ones that survive may live 50 years or more and have hundreds of offspring of their own.

Only about 1 in 100 crocodiles lives to be an adult

Adult crocodiles spend a lot of their time just lying around. When they do move from one location to another—to find food or a mate, or to find a warmer or cooler spot—they usually crawl with their belly touching the ground. When they are getting out of the water or trying to step over something, they may walk with just their feet and tail touching the ground. In the water, crocodiles swim by moving their tail back and forth. They often stay **submerged** for 20 minutes or more.

Crocodiles can run surprisingly fast in short bursts **21**

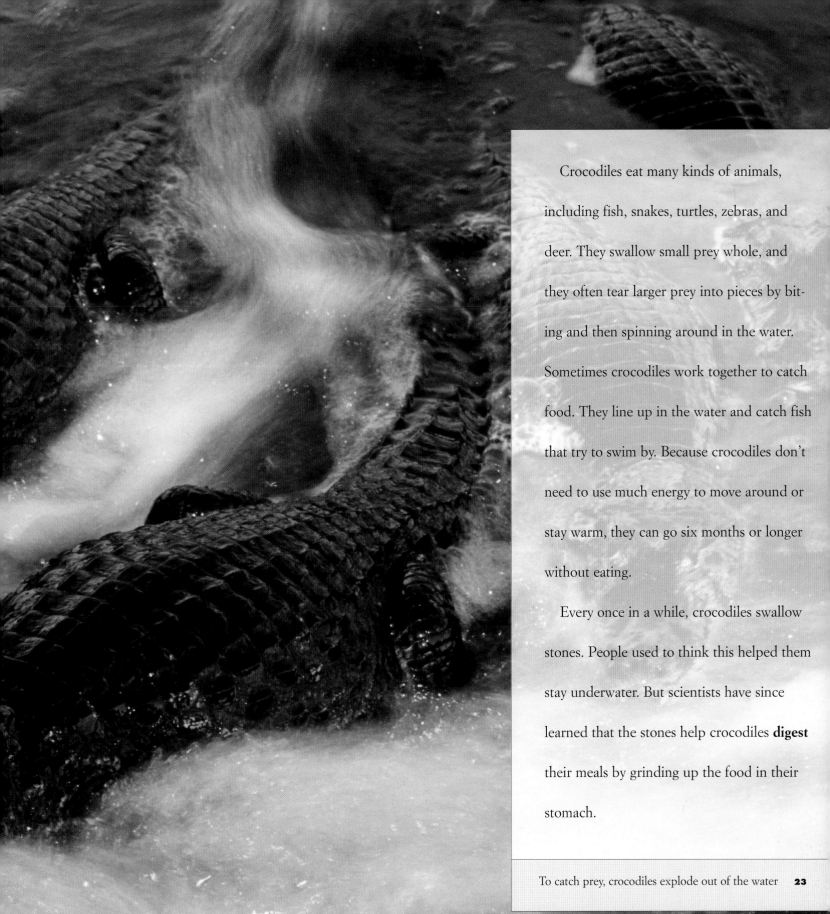

Crocodiles eat many kinds of animals, including fish, snakes, turtles, zebras, and deer. They swallow small prey whole, and they often tear larger prey into pieces by biting and then spinning around in the water. Sometimes crocodiles work together to catch food. They line up in the water and catch fish that try to swim by. Because crocodiles don't need to use much energy to move around or stay warm, they can go six months or longer without eating.

Every once in a while, crocodiles swallow stones. People used to think this helped them stay underwater. But scientists have since learned that the stones help crocodiles **digest** their meals by grinding up the food in their stomach.

To catch prey, crocodiles explode out of the water **23**

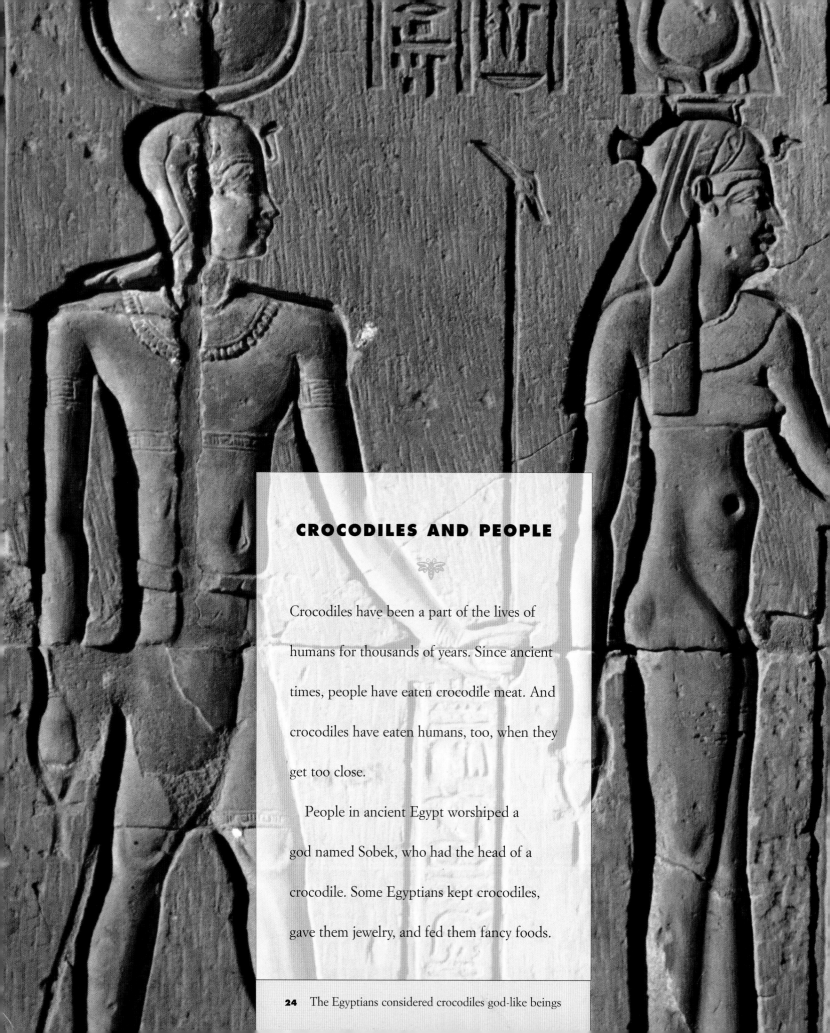

CROCODILES AND PEOPLE

Crocodiles have been a part of the lives of
humans for thousands of years. Since ancient
times, people have eaten crocodile meat. And
crocodiles have eaten humans, too, when they
get too close.

People in ancient Egypt worshiped a
god named Sobek, who had the head of a
crocodile. Some Egyptians kept crocodiles,
gave them jewelry, and fed them fancy foods.

Some crocodiles were made into mummies. There was even an Egyptian city called Crocodilopolis. Some Asian peoples also worshiped crocodiles.

In ancient Australia, **Aborigines** saw crocodiles as a symbol of strength. They told stories about crocodiles, such as how they got their teeth. The crocodile served as a **totem** for some groups of Aborigines. Many Aborigines believed that their ancestors took the form of a crocodile.

Two thousand years ago, Romans cap-
tured crocodiles and put them on display.
Today, zoos and wildlife exhibits around
the world still display crocodiles so people
can see them. Some entertainers put on
shows in which they wrestle crocodiles in
front of audiences. Crocodiles are sometimes portrayed in books, plays, and movies
as evil or scary creatures. In the story *Peter
Pan*, a crocodile follows a pirate captain
and eventually eats him.

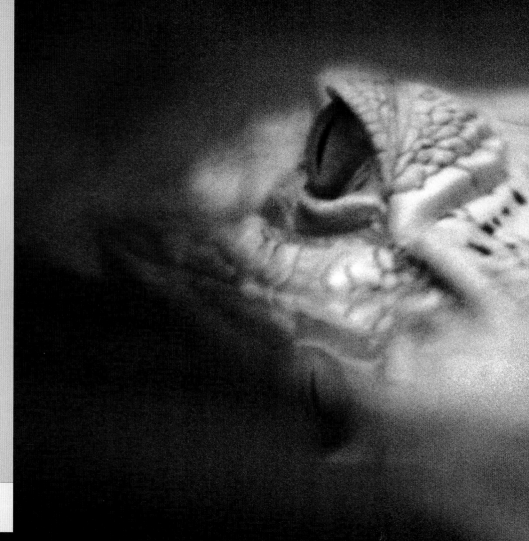

Crocodiles are often sneaky and dangerous in stories

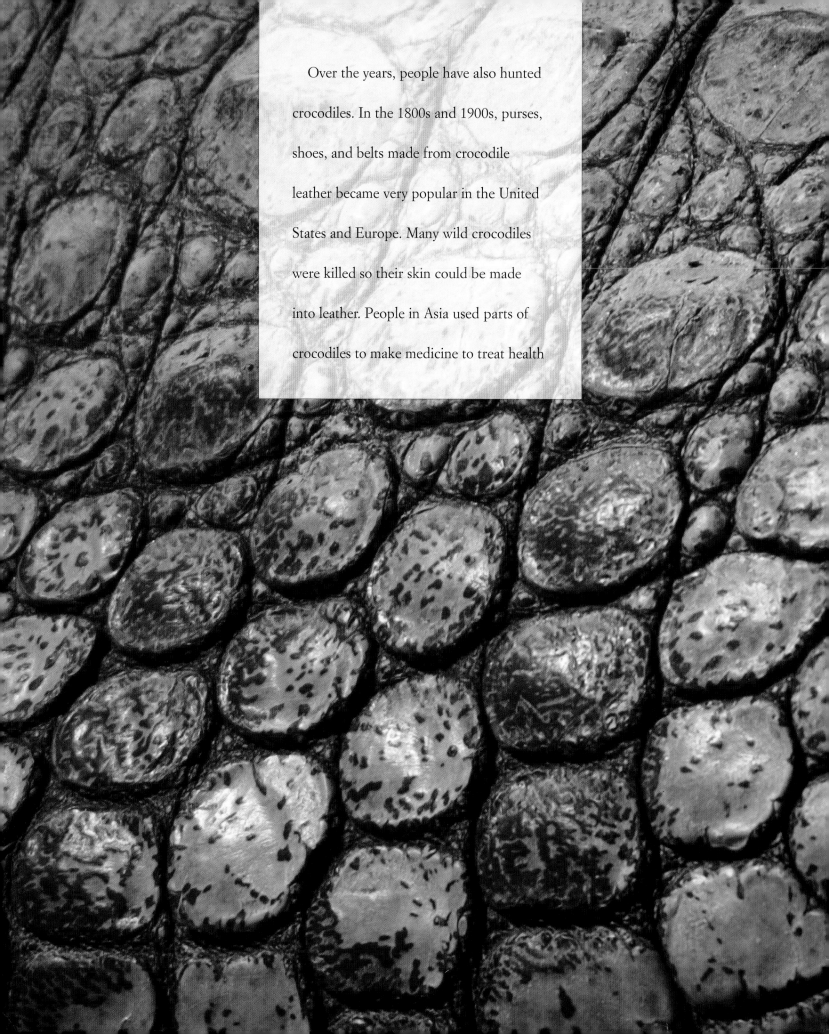

Over the years, people have also hunted
crocodiles. In the 1800s and 1900s, purses,
shoes, and belts made from crocodile
leather became very popular in the United
States and Europe. Many wild crocodiles
were killed so their skin could be made
into leather. People in Asia used parts of
crocodiles to make medicine to treat health

problems such as asthma. Other croco-

diles were killed for food or fun, or simply

because they were disliked. Eventually,

most crocodile species became **endangered**.

Many countries have passed laws protect-

ing crocodiles, and the number of wild

crocodiles has grown again. But in some

countries, they are still endangered.

Crocodile skin is very tough—and durable as clothing **29**

Today, people in Australia and other countries raise crocodiles on farms and ranches. They sell the crocodiles' skin for leather and their meat for food. Crocodile farming helps keep people from hunting wild crocodiles. Many people in Australia, Africa, and other areas are working today to make sure that crocodiles and the **habitat** in which they live are protected. Their efforts will help these huge, water-loving reptiles remain an important part of the wild world for many years to come.

Some people call crocodiles the last of the dinosaurs   31

GLOSSARY

Aborigines are dark-skinned, native people of Australia.

Adaptations are features of a living thing that help it survive where it lives.

When animals **digest** food, their bodies break it down so they can use the energy it provides.

An **endangered** animal is one that is at risk of dying off so that it no longer exists on Earth.

The place where a creature lives is called its **habitat**.

Mammals are animals that depend on milk for food when they are young.

Prey animals are animals that are caught and eaten by other animals.

When an animal **propels** itself, it uses its body to move in one direction or another.

Snakes, lizards, turtles, and crocodiles are all **reptiles**. Reptiles are cold-blooded and have scaly skin.

Some animals are divided into different kinds, or **species**. Members of a species can have young together.

When something is **submerged** in water, it is completely beneath the surface.

A **totem** is an animal or object that a person or group of people consider to be a symbol.

BOOKS

London, Jonathan. *Crocodile: Disappearing Dragon.* Cambridge, Mass: Candlewick Press, 2001.

Perry, Phyllis J. *The Crocodilians: Reminders of the Age of Dinosaurs.* New York: Franklin Watts, 1997.

Welsbacher, Anne. *Crocodiles.* Mankato, Minn.: Capstone Press, 2003.

WEB SITES

Animal Planet http://animal.discovery.com/convergence/safari/crocs/crocs.html

Crocodilians: Natural History and Conservation http://www.crocodilian.com

National Geographic.com Kids http://www.nationalgeographic.com/kids/creature_feature/0107/crocodiles.html

INDEX